Twenty Plus One – Poetic Reveries

Dr. Shivani Parikh

BookLeaf Publishing

India | USA | UK

Presentation by *BookLeaf Publishing*

Web: www.bookleafpub.com

E-mail: info@bookleafpub.com

ISBN: 9789363318458

First edition 2024

|| ओम् तत् सत् ||

[Om Tat Sat]

To The Absolute Truth

ACKNOWLEDGEMENT

I am very grateful to the publishers and editors for this unique opportunity given to me, and for their steadfast support and guidance that have made it possible for the book to be here.

I must thank my parents for their encouragement throughout the journey of this book. To my mom, Jignasa Parikh, I owe the understanding that a kind heart is not the opposite of a courageous one; rather, it is through courage and strength that true kindness and love are born. Special thanks to my dad, Dr. Brijesh Parikh, whom I pestered for criticism and insights after writing each poem. His insights and enthusiasm for my endeavors helped me stay motivated.

This book would not be here if not for the muses that constantly inspire me, from the abstract – nature, time, life, or death – to the many people that I know or have known, and especially my cat Felix.

It has always been said that a book shouldn't be judged by its cover, but a captivating cover never does any harm to a good book! I owe it to my talented and charming cousin, Hemansi Bhalani, for breathing life into my vision for the cover page of this book.

And last but, definitely not the least, I would like to thank you, dear reader, for having shown your faith in me and giving this book a chance to lead you into a world that existed only in my brain.

Much Love and Gratitude,
Shivani.

PREFACE

Dear divers,

Welcome to "Twenty Plus One – Poetic Reveries." In this preface, I invite you to explore the journey and purpose behind this work, aiming to provide insight into its creation and intentions.

I, Dr. Shivani Parikh, a Pathologist, embarked on the journey to create this book with the wish to explore my literary capabilities. This compilation of poems is an attempt to create a window that can invite in, the gentle breeze of life's varied emotions. It is also an attempt to leave a footprint of my existence apart from the prefix to my name. I absolutely love and adore my profession, but as Friedrich Nietzsche has said, "Life beats down and crushes the soul and art reminds you that you have one."

This book is therefore an attempt to create a niche, just as the reefs in the ocean do. Where one can dive in from time to time, escaping the chaos of the land and exploring the colors and vibrancy of emotion. Add to that a little whimsy and my love for numbers and the game of Scrabble, and this book gets its form.

This book is part of a 21-day challenge, and I, like most other instances in life, enrolled on the very last day. I therefore did not have a single day more. Hence, to celebrate the number '21', the title of the book and the title of each poem totals 21 Scrabble points (or its multiple).

Through the journey, my family and friends have been a constant inspiration, and of them, the following message by my dear masi, Meera Bhalani, has helped me believe in myself:

"In your words, a world unfurls,
A tapestry of dreams & pearls.
Each verse is a whisper, soft & true,
A glimpse of life seen through you.

Your poems dance like morning light,
Turning shadows into bright.
Keep writing; let your spirit soar,
For your words will open doors."

Bearing this beautiful poem in mind, I have approached writing poems for this book and poured all my heart and soul into it.

As you read this collection, may you find inspiration, comfort, and a deeper appreciation for the world around you. I hope you enjoy diving into this book on your own or reading it out loud to others, as much as I have loved to write it.

Love,
Shivani

ONE$_3$ – BEZOARS$_{18}$

(**Bezoar** = a small stony concretion which may
form in the stomachs of certain animals,
especially ruminants, and which was once used
as an antidote for various ailments)

Bezoars can ail and distress, forming in one's
Esophagus or gut, making one
Zestless due to pain, puking, and whatnot!
Oxen bezoars – prized possessions!
Antidote to arsenic; Symbol of wealth and
power;
Rare and mystical, a healer's charm…
She – the rare bezoar, indeed; him, the ailing ox.

TWO$_6$ – COMFY$_{15}$

(**Comfy** = comfortable)

Come, let's set camp here.
On grassy hills, under the
Milky Way; with mugs
Full of coffee. I'm all ears –
Yell, sigh; make your soul comfy.

THREE$_8$ – DETOX$_{13}$

(**Detox** = abstain from or rid oneself of toxic or
unhealthy substances)

Doughnuts and muffins in my dream,
Espresso with two sugars and some cream!
Today was a long day…
One indulgence is okay!
'Xpect me not to go to an extreme.

Dried flowers and scented candles,
Eau de parfums and oils made from sandal;
These calm the nerves, at once.
Oh no! not an indulgence!
'Xcept, if you can't handle.

Décor and aesthetics; chandeliers and glasses.
Exhilarating jewellery, gowns, and accessories;
These are objects of beauty
Only an innocent one would consider it haughty!
'Xpect me not to give up those vases!

Drums, guitars, and pianos; in my ear;
Every moment needs the music I hear.
The wind and the tree leaves – I have never really heard
On each tree, silent sits the bird.
'Xcept, if there's nothing already in my ear.

Donned in the finest silk and plush boots,
Evening creams and spas for hair roots.
To feel life through one's fingertips!
Of course, and the skinny dips!
'Xpect no one to give up on such lively loots.

FOUR$_7$ – FLUX$_{14}$

(**Flux** = the action or process of flowing)

Forward, we move, carrying our boulders,
Letting the tiny grains of sand dislodge and slip
by us.
Drooped sometimes and high from time to time,
our shoulders –
Marching forth in the flux of time with a lot of
fuss.

Letting the tiny grains of sand dislodge and slip
by us,
Unaware of their precious worth.
Marching forth in the flux of time with a lot of
fuss;
Alas! How we crushed all the bliss and mirth!

Unaware of their precious worth –
Xenotimes may be masked by the boulder
Alas! How we crushed all the bliss and mirth!
The gems that bring warmth when all else is
colder.

Xenotimes may be masked by the boulder
So, let's not miss out on the sands, brown, and
yellow –
The gems that bring warmth when all else is
colder
In the flux of time; are laughter and music
mellow.

FIVE$_{10}$ – GAMBIT$_{11}$

(**Gambit** = an act or remark that is calculated to gain an advantage, especially at the outset of a situation)

Gallantly, she strode, one bleeding foot in front of the other;
Marking the black soil crimson, one step after another.

Approaching doom as if it were nothing more than a child's play,
Yielding one sword in each hand, as if it were as light as hay.

Making way for her meagre yet mighty troop to
infiltrate
Right into the heart of the sea of foes knocking
on their gate.

Blocking the enemy, bleeding profusely, yet the
serene smile?
Does she not know that death is on his way,
away just a mile?

Injured flesh and an intact spirit – how fierce!
The win was a cinch!
Losing was never an option; for sacrifice – there
wasn't a flinch.

To watch your land be safe as you sigh goodbye
to life
Ah! To send your rivals to greet death before
entering the afterlife!

SIX$_{10}$ – HAUNTED$_{11}$

(**Haunted** = frequented by a ghost or showing signs of mental anguish or torment)

Happy-go-lucky. Hopping about with pigtails swaying side to side;
Amber-eyed, pale as paper, skinny to the bones and wearing hair bows.
Undetected by the public eye, whistling like the tune of silent tides;
Now here and soon there, rustling the fallen leaves as she goes.
Talking to the wind, tales of old days: When she was not yet stabbed for an
Emerald on her neck. Pretty shoes soiled by blood and not the garden soil of Jan
Death came too early for her, for long had greed haunted the madman.

SEVEN$_8$ – JESTER$_{13}$

(**Jester** = a professional joker or 'fool' at a
medieval court)

"Who is a jester?" questioned the child, curious
as a cat,
"The man with odd boots, dressed in yellow
with polka dots?"
Impatient fingers fidgeting; yet eyes not once
did he bat
For the old man sat in silence, still deep in his
thoughts.

"He amuses; smiles, cries, jumps about, and
makes silly noises
People laugh, bewildered and charmed, thinking
him bereft of wits.
But surely you knew of him, his antics, and how
the crowd rejoices.
What intrigues you: his ramblings and actions or
the garment he flits?"

"The purpose," declared the child with utmost
nonchalance.
Eyes twinkling and a smile playing at the corner
of his lips,
The old man stood at once, his staff a prop for
balance;
Scratching his silver chin, hand resting on his
hips.

"He is the messenger of the Lords, prodding
each to think of this:
Do the lives we live differ much from any jests
of his?"

EIGHT$_9$ – KLEPTO$_{12}$

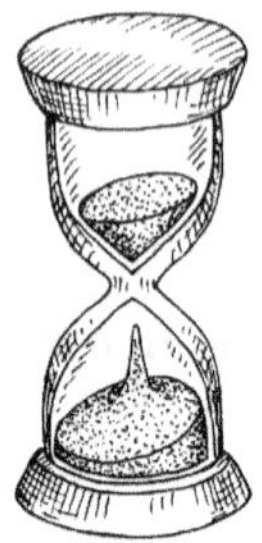

(**Klepto** = (Kleptomaniac) Someone who has a compulsion to steal)

Kettle on the stove, whistling away, up the lid goes
The steam making shapes through its long nose;
Amusing the young eyes! Tiny hands go clap – clap,
Time is nascent, laughter abounds! Tiny feet go tap – tap.

Long strides, longer lines, lots to learn; friends and foes
Making, breaking, keeping up, and walking on tippy toes.
Jokes and somersaults all around. Why would you nap,
When time is growing up so fast, moving with a zap!

Exams and goals are new on the block. Talent shows
And sports to focus on. Look how laughter flows: Snorts and a guffaw to chuckles and giggles, in a snap
Have been changed by the time that is taking a lap.

Parents to please and bosses to impress, I suppose;
Time has made giggles rare and invited more woes.
Laughter, now a restless bird whose wings go flap – flap
Or is it lost, having misread the lines on a map?

Tomorrow to be planned, yesterday still on pause
In the film, which in the mind, on and on goes.
Forward and rewind, the present just a gap
With a monotone and scattered smiles as a wrap

Old and wise, being present; life is nearing its close
Flashbacks, wondering about the highs and lows;
Where did all the laughs go, slowly? Oh Crap!
Time had been a Klepto! Laughter a bird in his trap!

NINE$_4$ – LIZARDS$_{17}$

(**Lizard** = a small reptile that has a long body,
four short legs, a long tail, and thick skin;
simply put, just YUCK!)

Lizards are such a… "yuck!"
With their stony eyes
And coarse, 'icky' skin,
Short limbs and sharp nails;
Giving me the shivers,
Cold, sweaty palms, and
The heebie-jeebies!

Crawling and hiding,
Wracking my nerves,
My fear knows no bounds.
My cat is amused,
He pretends to hunt,
Pouncing and darting around.
Enough with the heebie-jeebies!

But he, too, is scared,
I am sure.
Though I would much rather
He kept meowing,
Instead of tearing
Into the lizard's tail.
Heebie-jeebies again!

Oh God! Why won't it just leave?
Let me be at peace,
Enough! Enough!
No longer can I look
At this creature, and
No longer can I write about it,
Without having the heebie-jeebies!

TEN$_3$ – MIXTAPE$_{18}$

(**Mixtape** = a compilation of favorite pieces of
music, recorded on a tape, or another medium by
an individual)

If I would have had a chance –
I would make you a mixtape.
Not with the songs we heard on loop,
Not even with the ones we cried to;
But a mixtape of the songs we sang badly.

If I would have had a chance –
I would make you a mixtape.
Not of your favorite songs; nor mine,
And certainly not the ones we hated;
But of the sound of our laughter to silly jokes.

If I would have had a chance –
I would make you a mixtape.
Not of the debates or issues we talked of,
Not even the dialogues that intrigued us;
But of the transcripts of unsaid words lost to us.

If I would have had a chance –
I would make you a mixtape.
Not of the birdsongs or thunderstorms,
Not even the instrumentals that calmed us;
But of the stories that our eyes told our deaf
ears.

If I would have had a chance –
I would make you a mixtape.
I would play it on loop, just checking;
Wrap it up in silver and red;
And yet never really give it to you.

ELEVEN$_9$ – NECROTIC$_{12}$

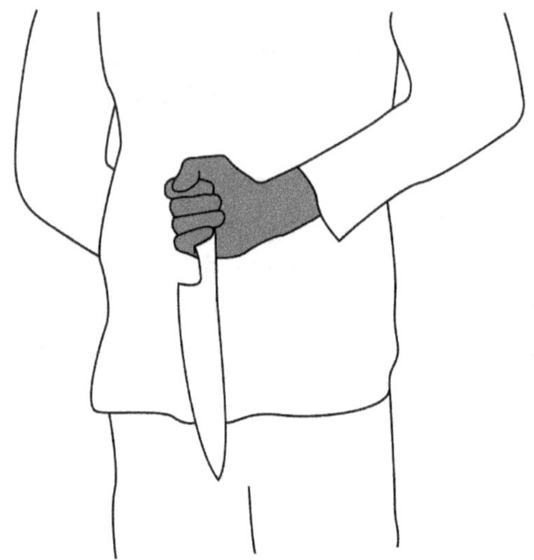

(**Necrotic** = affected with, characterized by, or producing death of a usually localized area of living tissue)

Not days, nor weeks, and not mere months'
concerns;
Two whole years were spent whilst nursing
those burns
That seemed to be self-inflicted. Oh! How
careless!
Pity! To have lived and relived in the memory, I
fess!

Brutal it was! For what kills the piglets first…
The knife?
Or to the sight of the yielding hand, they thought
gave them life?
To have known it as a gentle respite and now
Death's scythe,
Pity! How nice if the mind could go numb and
be blithe!

Painful, to watch hands scorched by the soup
they brewed.
Behold! Those that were fed have employed a
scheme so rude!
How naïve to go about baring your soul's real,
yet rough surface,
For isn't the world used to facades and a vary of
real faces?

Pain! The necrotic tissue now covered with
wrinkled skin,
Stinging, burning, stinking, and the liquid-y
mess within.
Dried up, eventually; leaving behind souvenirs
of fibrosis –
Repair demands abolition of the rotten, for a
better prognosis.

The maps of the memory ask me at times: "Was it wise –
To breathe life into something only to watch its demise?"
"Necrosed and healed; the scars are a tribute to the potential
And hope of finding the courage to do what is essential."

TWELVE$_{12}$ – PUPIL$_9$

(**Pupil** = black opening in the middle of the
colored part of the eye)

Facing the mirror;
Noticing splashes and spots,
De-silvered edges,
Missing stones adorning it
And tiny cracks, just forming.

Hair flying and free,
Oh! Look at those grey ones
Behind boastful black
All bouncing, flying around
In the gentle summer breeze.

Now the ageing lines
Around the eyes, deepening;
The tiny freckle
At the side of the forehead,
Still unchanged and unyielding.

Upturned curvature
Of the tiny old lips, and
Pits on glassy cheeks;
The amusement they express
And the stories they can tell!

But that is not all;
To quieten the chaos
Stop! Wandering eyes
Must now find themselves. Focus!
Into the tiny black pond.

THIRTEEN$_{11}$ – Q$_{10}$

(Q = the 17th letter of the English alphabet)

If 'Q' were a person, surely she would be
boastful!
Leading almost three hundred and never not
useful.

To stand alone and to mean 'a female monarch'
Or 'something that seeks information' with a
mark.

How rare to lead those few, of which most are
elite, exquisite;
'Qabalah', 'quagga', 'quagmire', 'quantum',
'quark', 'quartz', isn't it?

Wait! There's more: 'Queen', 'quench', 'quest',
'quiche', and
There's 'quicksilver', 'quintessential', 'quinoa',
'quote'; the end?

Not 'quite'! Ahem! Pardon such indulgences of
mine
For, awed I am, at the possibilities of the words
so fine.

To announce emotions varied, from anger and
zest in 'quarrel'
And peace as tranquility in 'quiet'. Yes, I
promise an end with a moral!

Even if it all sounds 'quixotic', much
amazement is due
At how 'Q' is everything in 'Queue', but almost
nothing without 'u'.

FOURTEEN$_{11}$ – RECIPE$_{10}$

(**Recipe** = a set of instructions for preparing a
particular dish, including a list of the ingredients
required)

Nutritious and scrumptious,
Fit for an insatiable zeal;
To prepare 4 servings of 'Presumptuous'
Follow the recipe; no big deal!

You will need:
Four cups of overconfidence
Two teaspoons real ignorance, to knead
With 150 ml of arrogance.

Don't you forget,
Five slices of disregard, so keen
Two chopped 'never-regret',
And a pinch of cunning, pristine!

Blend and boil to a steaming stew,
In the discomfort of the unwitting prey,
Once chilled, apply some sour rue,
Mold it as a decree, lead it astray.

Serve it cold, with an air of pomp;
Witness the feaster quiver;
And be done with it in a chomp,
And let them shudder and shiver.

FIFTEEN$_{13}$ – SIMILE$_8$

(**Simile** = a figure of speech involving the
comparison of one thing with another thing of a
different kind)

I am surely fond of some alliteration,
With words working wonders where
Just one alphabet is in attention,
Like a captain of some army, on a mare.

Allusion – another arrow in the quiver.
Borrowing from the ghosts of the past –
A Midas touch to poem, it shall deliver
An impact of words, which since ages last.

Euphemism has always been the dearest,
Glorifying the only unchanging truth –
Something that makes mortal life the rarest
Giving purpose to the pursuits of youth.

Hyperbole is always more fun to write,
Adding glitter and spark to the lines as if –
The stars descended from the sky at night!
You see what I mean, right?

Onomatopoeia makes me visualize
An orchestra playing through the alphabet,
Boom! Clang! Ping! Swoop! And a baby's cries!
Pleasing at times and a horror if one lets.

But nothing is as elegant as a simile,
What else can so easily lure a child to poetry?
Even if this poem is as simple as a simile,
Aren't you tempted to write your own poetry?

SIXTEEN$_{14}$ – TRIAGE$_7$

(**Triage** = the process of determining the most
important people or things from amongst a large
number that require attention)

The room was a mess, but that was not new,
With objects aplenty and drawers, but a few.

But the warning had been issued and a target set,
For the trip to happen, it was a must to win the
bet.

Jumping around, figuring out the ins and outs,
Pile to pile, no clue! Here come the panic bouts!

Ok! Apply some tricks, and take it one sock at a
time,
Triage the piles, make a list, and drink some
lime.

Socks first, shirts next, and skirts at the end,
Step by step, make haste! Respect the running
sand!

Three hours, not a hefty price to pay,
For months' worth of clutter to be swept away.

The challenge was to be won, no doubt,
Fun, frolic, and the joy to dance about!

The trip was the proclaimed prize, agreed,
But the real win was the space now freed!

SEVENTEEN$_{12}$ – VICE$_9$

(**Vice** = a weakness of character or behavior; a
bad habit)

Every cloud must have silver lining,
Every sunset must bring a new morning.
There is always a little white light
In the dark and deep, pitch-black night,
And we must cling to it with all our might.

Why, then, can we not tolerate
A speck of dust on a glass plate?
Why does a pimple make us uneasy?
The pus making our stomachs queasy,
For we expect life to be easy and breezy!

Come, breathe with me, in and out;
Hold your anger, sorrow, and self-doubt
See them as glass tile in a mosaic – you!
Look at the tiny pebble in the shoe,
Wait with patience in a long queue.

Virtues have been hailed for good,
Rules and rhymes follow, you should!
But cut some slack for your own sake!
Vices are stepping stones for wisdom's sake,
Guiding us through lessons we must partake.

So next time you see that anger seething,
Making you ail like a baby who's teething
Think of this vice, not as a monster, eerie;
Don't loathe or make yourself weary,
Let it pass and think of something cheery.

EIGHTEEN$_{12}$ – WORDS$_9$

(**Word** = single, distinct, meaningful elements of
speech or writing)

If only the words came easy!
And the job would be done without being
cheesy.

I am absolutely at a loss for thoughts,
My creativity seems to have gone for a toss.

The pages are blank, and so in my brain,
All the conjectures seem so lame and in vain.

The single spot of ink that fell from the pen,
Is now black and all dried up, and since when!

If this is what it is to be, why not let it all go,
Blow out the lamps, drop the curtain, and take a
bow.

For the story may not be over,
But the scene can be cut and done over.

Splash some water on your face, sip your tea,
Have a cookie and just let it be.

For the words have a wish of their own,
Magic happens when you relax and all control is
gone!

NINETEEN$_8$ – XENIAL$_{13}$

(**Xenial** = friendly, especially to guests or
strangers; describes hospitality and the warm,
welcoming treatment of visitors)

The plane was obscured by winds that were
whirling,
The thunder had masked the engine's whirring,
Safe had been their landing on a land unknown
Far away from the one they call their own.

Fate had been cold and blood had flooded
The lanes of the cities they inhabited.
"Refugees" was their new identity
Survival, self-preservation: the prime necessity.

Gunshots had driven them away from home,
But persistent biases made it harder to roam
The new lanes they had yet to explore
Whilst holding at heart their old lore.

Pastries and pies were abundant here,
But they longed for simpler soups, held dear.
The setting sun brought back the eyes' dew
That the rush of the day hid from others' view.

Gratitude that did express, surely!
To the new abode that was becoming theirs,
slowly.
Far and wide was it known to be the most xenial
Yet! Home it was not, any denial?

TWENTY$_{12}$ – YANTRA$_9$

(**Yantra** = [Sanskrit] instrument or machine; a geometrical diagram, or any object, used as an aid to meditation)

This ancient wisdom implores us to harness focus,
Teaching and preaching the marvels in a single locus.

Asking you to see the world around for what it is,
And let your Self free from what your mind perceives.

"Draw a bindu within patient lines, on a parchment,
Connect with your Self and practice detachment.

Take some time out of the hustle and bustle,
Listen to the wind's whisper and the birds' whistle.

Take the simplest yantra or the most complex,
It is designed to elevate, never meant to be a
hex.

Millions have gone and millions will elapse,
Alas! Years, months, and moments; all collapse!

Why bother for fleeting fineries of the flasks
When one can drink from the fountain
immortal?" It asks

Sacred is the wisdom that fills moments with life
Scared are those who wish to cram time into life.

TWENTY$_{12}$ PLUS$_6$ ONE$_3$ – ZAPPY$_{21}$

(**Zappy** = lively, energetic)

Zigzagging around,
Attack on plush mouse's tail!
Pawing at its head –
Pouncing – hiding – and repeat
Yay! Look at the zappy cat!

www.ingramcontent.com/pod-product-compliance
Lightning Source LLC
La Vergne TN
LVHW021308200726
843509LV00012B/1841